Welcome to the world of Anne Geddes.

The images used in this journal are taken from Anne's latest collective work entitled *Down in the Garden*.

Anne says in her foreword to that book:
"I hope that, through my work as a photographer, I have been able to pass on my appreciation of the beauty and charm of little children. As adults we all need to stop occasionally and look at ourselves and our circumstances with an open mind and a sense of humor, and remember to appreciate the simple things in life, which are often the most important."

We hope that when using this journal you can record some of the simple, yet magic, moments of your life's journey.

Greetings friend~

Endings & new beginnings. We have been through many. Death and rebirth, they have been our companion and teacher. The butterfly child reminds me of the newness of life and the possibilities of each day. The child in me awakens a bit more each day, laying aside the seriousness for the play; the challenge for the joy. I want to allow more joy in my life ~ you have always been like the flower from which nectar can be sipped! Thanks for spreading joy, childlike innocence and laughter!

Dear Susan E.,

I have always loved words and images. Nothing conjures up in my mind more images of you than children. What joy you have touched the world with and given birth to. And thanks for helping me keep the child alive in me!

I want to share with you different writing ~ things that have touched my soul. I pray they enrich your journey and cause you to reflect on the "simple things in life which are often the most important." Happy 44th!

Love,
Susan R.

ANNE GEDDES

Down in the Garden

Journal

ANNE GEDDES ™

ISBN 0-7683-2042-9

© Anne Geddes 1996

First published in 1996 by Hodder Moa Beckett Publishers

Published in 1997 by Photogenique Publishers
(a division of Hodder Moa Beckett)
Studio 3.16, Axis Building, 1 Cleveland Road, Parnell
Auckland, New Zealand

First USA edition published in 1996 by Cedco Publishing Company,
100 Pelican Way, San Rafael, CA 94901

This edition published in 1998.
10 9 8 7 6 5 4 3 2 1
Designed by Jane Seabrook
Produced by Kel Geddes
Color separations by Image Centre
Images first published in *Down in the Garden*

Printed by Midas Printing Limited, Hong Kong

Please write to us for a FREE FULL COLOR catalog of our fine
Anne Geddes calendars and books, Cedco Publishing Company,
100 Pelican Way, San Rafael, CA 94901.
or, visit our website : www.cedco.com

"even though... parts of ourselves are still underground, our spirituality is taking root, growing and pushing through to life. In its own time, when the pregnancy is completed, it will emerge from hiddenness."

—maria harris

what is giving birth, growing in you?

Canterbury Belles

"I wish I'd known from the beginning that I was a strong woman! What a difference it would have made! I wish I had known that I was born a courageous woman; I've spent so much of my life cowering. How many conversations would I not only have started but finished? If only I'd known I possessed a warrior's heart? I wish I'd known that I'd been born to take on the world; I wouldn't have run from it for so long, but run to it with open arms."

~ Sarah Ban Breathnach

And not merely to know that we were strong, but that it was o.k.! And indeed I sense some days my friend~ we have taken on the world! It's knocked us on our butts several times, but we always seem to get back up again! Thank god!

Susan R.

SURPRISE!!

Savor the unexpected...

when SLEEPING BEAUTY wakes up,
she is almost fifty years old.
                    —maxine kumin

the word intimacy comes from a Latin root that means innermost.

— Susan Wittig Albert

In our most precious relationships, we trust the other person enough to reveal our innermost selves. And we can provide that safety and nourishment for others.

Psychologist Carl Jung wrote, " the meeting of two personalities is like the contact of two chemical substances: if there is any reaction, both are transformed!"

We have been blessed with great transformation. What a joy to see you move through so many places: D.J., school, jobs, Mike, children, friendships, John. You are an incredibly talented woman — what a joy + privilege I have to call you friend. Your laughter has sustained me; your prayers held me; your strength lifted me up! ♫

What do you plan to
do with your own
wild and precious
life?
                            -mary Oliver

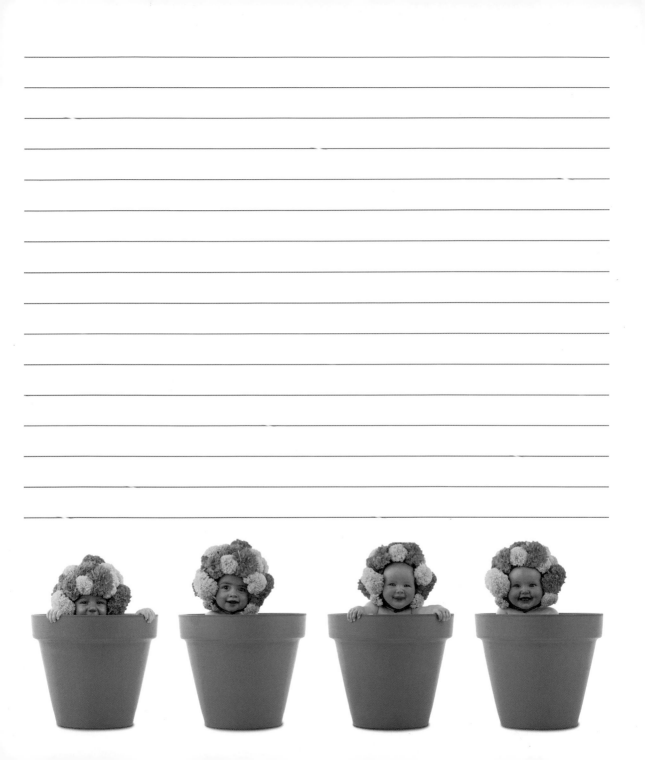

Out of the strain of the
Doing,

Into the peace of the
Done.
～Julia Louise Woodruff

Take time to rest and celebrate!

The plots of God

and Love are one

and the same thing.

-Niall Williams

If ambition doesn't
hurt you,
you haven't got it!

~Kathleen Norris

Like any art,
the creation of self
is both natural and
seemingly impossible!
It requires training
as well as
MAGIC

—holly near

Have a young soul ... be young at
heart. The thirteenth century German
mystic wrote:
My soul is as young as the
day it was created.
Yes! And much younger!
In fact, I am younger today
than I was yesterday
and if I am not younger tomorrow
than I am today
I shall be ashamed of myself.
People who dwell in God
dwell in the eternal Now.
There, people can never grow old.
There, everything is present
and everything is new!

A strong woman is a woman
who loves strongly
and weeps strongly
and is strongly terrified
and has strong needs.
—Marge Piercy

ACT,
AND GOD
WILL
ACT!

-Joan of Arc

hope is a

very unruly

emotion...

(always popping up out of
thin air!)

(never give in to despair)

To be of the Earth is to know
the restlessness of being a seed
the darkness of being planted
the struggle toward the light
the pain of growth into the light
the joy of bursting and bearing fruit
the love of being food for someone else
the scattering of your seeds
the decay of the seasons
the mystery of death
the miracle of birth

                              —John Soos

We shall not cease from exploration.

and the end of all our exploring

will be to arrive where we started.

and know the place for the first time.

-t.s. eliot